The Poetry Of an Ordinary Life

by

Wendy Grace Stevens

© 2016, Wendy Grace Stevens

Stevens, Wendy Grace
    The Poetry of an Ordinary Life / by Wendy Grace Stevens. I Street Press : Sacramento, CA 2016

ISBN: 978-1-941125-92-2

Library of Congress Control Number: 2016963003

I gratefully acknowledge the many loving friends who supported and encouraged my writing. Special thanks to Christine Begovich and Jim Hargrove, who were there for me every step of the way, and to Carol McKenzie, Ph.D, who gave her time and expertise to edit this work. My heartfelt thanks to each of you.

Cover photograph by Wendy Grace Stevens
Cover designed and created by Jim Hargrove.

Introduction 1
    The Late Night Poet 3
    My Poetic Child 4

Section I

The Poetry of an Ordinary Life 5
    Compassionate Fog 7
    Spring of my Soul 8
    Sweet Release 9
    Someday 10
    Lean in and Listen 12
    The Poetry of an Ordinary Life 13
    Speak Out for Peace 14
    Shine 15
    Creativity 16

Section II

Observations 17
    La Sonambula 19
    Culture Clash at the Nail Salon 20
    Wheels 21
    Perceptions 22
    Incident at the Market 23
    Spare Parts 24

Section III

The Poetry of Nature 25
    The Red Bench 27

    Footprints in the Dunes 28

    Moonlight Musings 29

    Blessing from the Sea 30

    Clouds 31

    Seventeen Mile Drive 32

    Waiting for the Moon 33

    Richard's Poem 34

    Leaving Taos 35

Section IV

Of Love and Longing 37

    Love Is 39

    Moments 40

    Somewhere in the Night 41

    Text Gone Wild 42

    On the Night of the Eclipse 44

    The Road to Nowhere 45

    I'm Choosing Me 46

    Intoxication 47

    No One Hears the Scream 48

    Love's Trance 49

Section V

Celebration and Loss 51

    Winter Solstice 53

    Thanksgiving Celebration 54

    Christmas Jam 56

Letter to Santa 58
Christmas Surprise 59
Mrs. C.'s Funeral 60
Wearable Hugs 61
Remembrance 62

Section VI
The Spirituality of An Ordinary LIfe 63
Was That You, God?... 65
God's Kite 66
Personal GPS 67
What Is God?.. 68
Beginner's Mind 69
Truth or Fiction 70
The Forest of My Mind... 72

Section VII
Just for Grins 75
Temptation... 77
An Ode to Dust... 78
Catatonic 80
The Daze of My Lies 81
Woman's Work is Never Done... 82
Cat in the Windowsill 83
Ideal Dinner Party 84
Cajun Tom 85

Introduction

The Late Night Poet

I did not set out to become a poet,
but once poetry took hold of me,
I've been compelled to write
about most anything I feel or see.

Sometimes my words come out funny,
all wrapped up in laughter.
Sometimes they're more like fairy tales,
ending in "happily ever after."

Poems spill from my funny bone,
or fly off the top of my head,
or are born deep within my heart,
not thought, by emotion only fed.

Wherever the words originate,
whether humorous or sincere,
my hope is that they'll convey
inspiration, comfort, or cheer.

Poems may ring of wisdom or wit,
or recall memories from the past.
But the most compelling reason I write
is to let my Self be known to Me at last.

My Poetic Child

Poetry, the child of my heart,
Born through my pen,
Ink its blood and rhythm its breath.

The desire to share is strong,
This tender and delicate child;
Yet the instinct to protect is stronger.

As a mother would not place her babe
In the arms of a stranger
Who may not care for and adore it,

Though I take pleasure and pride
In these writings that sometimes surprise me,
They remain secret, securely in their cradle.

Section I

The Poetry of an Ordinary Life

Compassionate Fog

Misty fog hangs above the river,
the few fishermen reduced to shadowy silhouettes
in the soft morning light.

The sun is weak and wan,
like the moon, a dimly glowing disk
floating in a pale sky.

Fog softens the contours of the landscape,
concealing usually obvious flaws,
lending an air of mystery to the familiar.

Might we take a cue from Nature,
view others through a slightly foggy veil,
see them more compassionately
and allow the mysteries of each soul to shine through?

Spring of my Soul

Winter's kill must be cleared away in preparation for Spring's new bloom.
As paint and soap renew my living space, so it is with my life.
The old and worn must be cleared away in anticipation of my personal Spring, a renewing of my body and soul.
I release things that no longer satisfy me and seek new rewards in friendships, community, and activities, in well-being and healthy habits.

I have traveled this road before, resisting change, clinging to what was, begging for stability, only to discover greater stability in accepting change.
New communities have arisen, new love has lifted me.
I have watched myself grow and blossom, discovering parts long hidden, strengths I never suspected.

Now is the time to trust those strengths, that love, that resilience and venture forth into my own new Spring, with my heart open to opportunities to grow, to bloom, and most of all, to love.
May I learn to be grateful for change, to anticipate its blessings, to give thanks for the unknown good that is sure to come.

Sweet Release

It seems I was born swaddled in fear,
but as life goes on, it's abundantly clear
that for every fear I finally release,
the more I feel my joy increase.

When I was young, I was so shy
I couldn't look another in the eye.
Now interactions reap sweet dividends.
Life truly begins at the place fear ends.

Someday

Beware of Someday, it's where
your dreams are sent to die.
You send them off with good intent,
but in the blinking of an eye
the lovely plans, the hopes you had,
the trips you vowed to take,
languish on the shores of Someday,
a fetid, lifeless lake.

Make friends with Meanwhile,
for that's where you can thrive.
It's where life unfolds,
while you wait for Someday to arrive
like a knight in shining armor
to turn your dreams to reality.
But dreams and knights and fairy tales
don't come true easily.

Gather your courage
and look Meanwhile squarely in the face.
Is there something you can do
to make Meanwhile a better place?

Can you summon back one small dream
or wish now and then?
The smallest dream, a tiny wish,
close to your heart again?

Realize Meanwhile is Now,
and All You've Got, and Today,
and call back those dreams,
before your Meanwhile slips away.
You don't want to be old,
sitting in your rocking chair,
with nothing to remember
but dreams that vanished in thin air.

Lifetimes lived in Meanwhile
are all we really experience.
So return your dreams to Meanwhile,
it's only common sense.
Refuse to consign the hopes
and plans and dreams you cherish
to the barren, alien world of Someday,
where they are sure to perish.

Lean in and Listen

Lean in, lean in and listen.
Hear what he says, he who you view as other.
Be not embarrassed by your interest.

Lean in, lean in and hear.
Her manner of dress is different from yours,
and you've never read that holy book she carries.

It takes courage to be different.
It takes courage to be open and inquiring.
Aren't you a little different?
Aren't you a little curious?

What common thread may bind you?
Do you not share the same needs?
Needs for dignity, respect, compassion?

Lean in, lean in and learn.
Perhaps wisdom can be shared.
Perhaps understanding can grow.
Perhaps friendship may occur.
Perhaps love may conquer.

The Poetry of an Ordinary Life

There is poetry in an ordinary life,
in the measured rhythm of its days.
The enchantment of each sunrise and sunset,
the wonder of changing seasons.
Time spent with friends in laughter,
the quiet solitude that restores the soul.
Times of learning and growing,
of loving and parting.
The poetry of a life's passions brought to fruition
and remembrance of dreams abandoned
or revised by the changing circumstances
of an ordinary life.
Each ordinary life has its ebb and flood,
just as the oceans do.
A heartbeat,
a pulse,
a rhythm,
a meaning,
a poem.

Speak Out for Peace

So much hateful talk!
So many acts of violence!
Speak out loud for peace.
It's no time for timid silence.

Angry voices rant and rage,
attempting passions to incite.
The voice for love, calm and soft,
speaks a future much more bright.

Remember you have power
and use it wisely in this pursuit.
It's up to every one of us
the tide of hatred to refute.

Shine

Does life disappoint because we ask too much of it?
Or because we ask too little of ourselves?
We're taught modesty is a virtue;
don't boast; wait your turn.
We dim our light.

No longer children, it's time to shine
and do what we came to do.
We each have a mountain to climb,
our own flag to fly, our own horn to blow.

Sing your song!
Dance as only you can!
Give your unique gift.
It's yours alone to give.

Creativity

The ancients believed that Genius Creativity
existed somewhere in the ethers with the proclivity
of seeking mortal beings through whom to express.
So when Inspiration visits you, just say "Yes!"

Though you may live like a chicken in a tiny coop,
you're really a majestic eagle that can soar and swoop.
Realize and refuse to hide your inborn majesty,
and synchronistic events will support your true identity.

Hiding your light benefits no man, woman, or child.
Let Genius express through you, go a little wild.
Let yourself sing and dance, write novels or paint.
Welcome Creative Genius without constraint.

For if Genius wanders looking for someone to bless,
mortals can't take all the credit for failure or success.
Perhaps we're visited by different Genies day to day,
and some know better what we'd agree to do or say.

Section II

Observations

La Sonambula
(The Sleepwalker)

In nightgown demure she walked the balcony above,
eyes closed in slumber, candle in outstretched hand.
He watched from the courtyard below and fell in love,
unaware she was betrothed to another man.

Enchanted by her beauty, knowing not even her name,
he climbed the stone steps to engage in her dance.
Soft kisses to her face lit by the candle's dim flame
caused her to awaken and flee his warm advance.

With tear-filled eyes, to the courtyard he descended.
Where spilt his tears grew a rose the color of her flame.
He sat in silent heartbreak, dreams of romance ended,
not knowing in her dreaming heart she felt the same.

Culture Clash at the Nail Salon

The greeter is a young Asian woman,
diminutive, soft-spoken and shy,
her long black hair overlaid
with powdered turquoise dye.

In one corner is an altar
bearing offerings of fruit and sweets
wrapped in brightly colored paper
inscribed with writing I can't read.

Two women watch the mute TV,
English subtitles on an Asian show,
while Sinatra's songs fill the room,
a curiously mixed tableau.

A young man is doing nails.
He wears an American Eagle t-shirt.
One arm is covered in tattoos;
in halting English he admits it hurt.

With the language and customs
of their new country they struggle.
While building new lives, learning
new ways, two cultures to juggle.

Wheels

A wobbly four-year-old rides her bike
tentatively down the sidewalk,
pink training wheels,
purple tassels on the handlebars,
imagining she's a teen-ager
flying along on a road bike.

A geezer speeds through the neighborhood
in his mid-life crisis, top down,
both hairs blowing in the wind,
attempting time travel back to his youth.

And the wheels of time inexorably turn.

Perceptions

The house is an eyesore, the neighborhood blight.
The yard is bare dirt, no vegetation in sight.
The people there raise rabbits, free range, no less.
One small black bunny had escaped through the mesh.

A teenage boy stood outside the fence, looking 'round,
ball cap backward, baggy pants dragging ground.
What mischief is he up to? I thought, as I came near.
When teenagers dress like that, intent is never clear.

Close enough to clearly see this tough-looking youth,
I realized I had completely missed the truth.
The boy was just a boy, dressed in his age's norm,
holding close the little bunny, keeping it safe from harm.

Incident at the Market

A young boy stood crying in the middle of the store.
He was a small child, about five, maybe only four.
His arms held a bear, well-loved and shabby.
Between tearful sobs he cried out for his daddy.

A kindly older woman came to his side,
kneeling to his level to look him in the eye.
"Did your daddy get lost?" she asked him brightly.
The boy hung his head and hugged the bear tightly.

"Do you think he's scared?" she soothingly asked.
"Perhaps we should look where you saw him last."
The child ceased wailing and thrust out his chin,
and earnestly said, "We've got to find him."

Off they went to rescue poor lost daddy dear,
hand-in-hand, the woman, the boy, and the bear.

Spare Parts

A litter of eight baby kittens
at the market to give away,
each one precious and adorable
in its own individual way.

Their colors and markings differed,
no two were even slightly a match.
It was hard to believe these kittens
all came from the same batch.

One kitty stood out from the rest,
and promptly won over my heart.
His unusual appearance looked as if
he was made out of leftover parts.

A snowy body with a long gray tail,
one ear black and two legs tabby-tan,
he looked for all the world as if he got
whatever spare parts were left on hand.

Section III

The Poetry of Nature

The Red Bench

At the top of the trail
leading up from the river
there's a little red bench,
its paint faded and peeling.
Yet its serene viewpoint
beckons invitingly to passersby.
Come, sit. Rest and linger
in quietness and reflection
or gratitude and joy.
Observe the river's easy flow,
the birds circling overhead,
the contrast of colorful fall leaves
against lush green grasses.
Breathe in the crisp autumn air.
Bask in the bright sunshine.
Soon it will be winter
and only snow will rest
on the little red bench.

Footprints in the Dunes

Arid, flat, sagebrush-clad desert,
harsh, devoid of interest.
Gold and yellow sand dunes
arise abruptly from the white ground
in stark contrast to the surrounding desert.
Immense featureless mounds,
until shifting light defines shadows,
illumines windswept ridges like ocean waves
or hair released from a braid.
Footprints trace intricate paths
across the desolate landscape.
Fleeting, temporal,
footprints don't last here.

Moonlight Musings

The full moon's light transforms my backyard
into a radiant wonderland.
The climbing rose waves welcome from its arbor.
All is shrouded in silent beauty.

Concrete sidewalks become silver pathways
leading to secret corners and unfamiliar vistas.
Camellia leaves glisten with reflected light.
White roses glow like eyes opened wide in awe.

Barefoot and clad for sleep,
I venture out through the bedroom door
to take in the shimmering beauty before me,
a cautious observer in a landscape of moonlit splendor.

Blessing from the Sea

Paddling in Monterey Bay, we felt disappointed
because we saw only gulls and raucous, smelly sea lions.
Then a single otter appeared among our loosely
clustered kayaks.
It swam silently from one boat to the next,
pausing to put its hands against each boat in turn,
staring into our faces with large, knowing eyes,
offering each of us a blessing from the Soul of the Sea.

Clouds

As I gaze through fall-colored trees
into October's light blue morning,
a pale half-moon hangs,
partly hidden by long, feathery clouds
rising from the western horizon.

O, to be a child again, lying in the grass,
finding pictures in the clouds.
But no, a child would miss the wonder.
A child might see a castle or a pony,
where I see the hand of God.

Seventeen Mile Drive
Monterey

A mystical, fog-shrouded forest --
An ethereal landscape where errant rays of sun
pierce the mist,
illumining occasional patches of brilliant grass.

Fairytale castles line the road,
Moorish palaces, towering spires,
sequestered in their private kingdoms.

Ocean vapors blend with the mist.
Wind-twisted cypress trees assume Halloween shapes.
Sentinel rocks withstand eons of incessant, crashing
waves.

Through it all, the heartbeat of Nature.

Waiting for the Moon

Come ye apart and rest a while.
Think on whatsoever is good,
whatsoever is lovely.
Awaiting moonrise above Yosemite Valley,
images of beauty surround.
Majestic waterfalls tumble far below,
filling the air with their music.
Brilliant pink clouds hover on the western horizon.
Evening's alpenglow creeps over Half Dome
as the sun's last rays tint towering walls of granite gold,
and the valley fades to shades of gray.
Quietly, gently, come ye apart and rest.

Richard's Poem

The last vestiges of a snowy winter
cling to the ridgetops,
slowly yielding to spring
as waterfalls and tumultuous streams
that nurture verdant meadows
and emerging wildflowers.
Lenticular clouds drift
across the afternoon sky,
an intense Maxfield Parrish-blue backdrop
for soaring granite peaks.

The photographer waits patiently
for just the right light,
the right cloud,
the defining shadow,
the perfect reflection.
Yet not even his discerning eye
nor technical expertise
can adequately capture
the magnificent beauty
of the Eastern Sierra landscape.

Leaving Taos

The full moon made a faint blur
in the overcast evening sky,
attempting in vain
to illuminate the snow-clad Rockies beneath.

The clouds closed over it
like a sleep-heavy eye,
and the mountains
pulled up the blanket of darkness
and went to sleep.

Section IV

Of Love and Longing

Love Is

Love is a dream,
    Seeking a heart
        In which to awaken.

Moments

How often have you heard ,
"Live for the moment," or "Be here now?"
No matter the current idiom,
it's a truth that merits attention.

It's much too easy to set love aside 'til later,
to concentrate on goals for the future,
on a time yet to come.

But we must remember, in the rush to achieve,
that life is made up of tiny moments---
one at a time,
one after another,
each unique,
and separate,
and never occurring again.
Yet stitched together,
they form the tapestry of life.

Each moment I spend with you
is my favorite moment, a sacred moment,
a moment I will cherish above all others.
I will treasure each moment we are together,
fully present and aware of our abiding love.

Somewhere in the Night

Did I dream, or were you there with me,
Holding me close, kissing my face,
Your body warmly curled around mine?
I don't remember you joining me
For an evening glass of wine,
Or feeling the bed move as you got in,
But you were there as I slept,
Somewhere in the night.

Did I dream, or were you really there,
Stroking my hair, whispering love,
Drawing me more tightly against you?
Never my dreams so warm and real,
Anointing my body with passion
Stretching into dawn's aloneness.
Let me return to slumber, to you,
Somewhere in the night.

Text Gone Wild

My Sweetheart sent a text today,
proclaiming his love and care.
Anyway, he said he did,
but it vanished in thin air.
Sent from his iPhone so smart,
where did that errant message go?
He looked again and saw the number
was one he didn't know.
I wondered who received that text
and what was their reaction.
It could have spurred a vast array
of misled interaction.

Was it a woman or man, a girl or boy?
Someone married, or hoping?
One whose last date disappointed,
who's spent a whole week moping?
Perchance a girl, too shy to smile
at the boy next door, blushes in delight.
Or a mother whose son stormed out
after an ordinary family fight.
Of course, it could have gone to one
where welcome it would not be.
A woman who thinks it came from one
whose interest she would flee.

A manly man who understands
the masculine tenor of that note.
Did he suspect his fishing buddy
and vow to toss him off the boat?

Oh, Sweetheart, let's hope your love note
landed on a soft, receptive heart,
and caused a loving chain reaction
that we can be proud to be a part.
From now on, Dearest, when sending
your tender thoughts by text,
be certain you're sending them to me,
not someone who'll be perplexed.

On the Night of the Eclipse

Late at night, as the world sleeps,
I explore the depths of my heart.
My mind relentlessly follows random thoughts
that lead me where they will,
but always back to you.
Like pictures in an old album,
scenes of our togetherness play
behind my eyes and across my heart.
Memories of us---do you remember, too?
The sights, the sounds, the flavors of new love?
Such an adventure, falling in love
at this late hour of life.
What will become of it?
When I'm with you, time stands still in my joy.
But alone, time seems scarce and precious as gold,
rushing to be with you again.
Like the moon emerging from eclipse,
the halo of love grows bigger, brighter, bolder,
until the sky is lit once more.
And so I wait, as the world slumbers,
to hear once more your voice at morning's light,
to say once more, "I love you."

The Road to Nowhere

If you're on the road to nowhere,
make sure to take the scenic byway.
When true love's a dead-end street,
why speed down the highway?

Enjoy the joys and pleasures
on love's sweet, wandering route.
When the bridge is burning behind you,
just bring the marshmallows out.

Revel in the present moment,
enjoy the taste of each sweet kiss.
Enfold your lover in tenderness,
and treasure true love's bliss.

Linger as long as you dare,
savor the beauty and delights,
for at your final destination
there'll be lonely, tear-filled nights.

I'm Choosing Me

Don't tell me how empty your life is.
Don't say how much you miss me.
Many times you could have chosen me,
but you chose otherwise.

Your life's not simple, you say.
Your schedule is demanding.
I'm through waiting
to be squeezed into odd moments,
the hidden, dusty corners of your life.

I'm not rejecting you; I'm choosing Me.
I'll buy myself a stunning ring
to wear on my left hand
to remind myself and everyone else
that I am choosing Me!

Intoxication

It's not the wine in my glass, lush and red,
Or the taste of it on my lips.
It *is* the morning breeze moving water.
Moonrise through clouds.
The first crisp days of autumn.
Sharing a decadent and delicious dessert.
Our love.

It isn't the unsteadiness of a little too much,
Or the giddiness of buying too-expensive shoes.
It *is* the experience of snowy mountains.
The far off song of an unseen singer.
A garden bursting with blooms.
Sitting together over morning coffee.
Our love.

It isn't the buzz from a heady Margarita,
Or winning big at a game of chance.
It *is* walking barefoot on soft grass.
Friends around the dining table.
Shafts of sunlight through the forest.
Falling into bed beside you.
Our love.

No One Hears the Scream

If I were alone on a desert island,
screaming from hunger or frustration,
no one would hear me scream
in the remoteness of my location.

Right where I am, I want to cry out
for your presence with anguished emotion,
but no one hears my heart scream
for reassurance of your devotion.

I dare not scream these things aloud,
feelings that remain hidden inside,
gnawing daily at my mind and heart
where thoughts of you constantly abide.

The scream is there, barely contained
behind the mask I allow the world to see,
but no one will ever hear the scream
because it's buried deep inside of me.

Love's Trance

In a room filled with sunlight,
lying with my cheek against
your bare shoulder,
not asleep, yet not awake,
dreamlike,
content in love's trance.

Section V

Celebration and Loss

Winter Solstice

Today is the first day of winter,
foggy and gray, with intermittent rain.
The unceasing breeze rings wind chimes
that hang from the patio rafters,
one cheery note in an otherwise bleak landscape.
There is no sign of life in my backyard, no birds,
no squirrels racing along the branches.

Recovering from a bout of dizziness and nausea,
I'm snuggled into a warm, soft, blue sweatshirt,
cautiously sipping a latte.
My first in days, it tastes delicious.

Sitting with old newspapers in front of the Christmas
tree, brightly lighted against the window's gloomy scene.
Not the gay Christmas depicted on Hallmark greetings,
but a peaceful awareness of returning health
and anticipation of returning light.

Thanksgiving Celebration

A friend invited me to
her Thanksgiving celebration.
I gladly said yes and offered
a culinary creation.
Salad would be great, she said,
one either fruit or green.
And here's where some restrictions
appeared upon the scene.

One son's a vegan, so don't use
butter, cream, or meat.
And no wheat, as Julie's family
gluten doesn't eat.
Unfortunately, Granny won't be there,
tears she's still shedding
because Jon and Debbie's baby
will arrive before their wedding.

Debbie will be there. Of course,
she refrains from drinking,
but Jon consumes her share, too.
What could he be thinking?

Marcia refuses wine not red;
Tom and Sarah drink only white.
Uncle Jim insists he has no use
for spirits of any type.

Beside a normal turkey perched
upon the festive table top
will rest a meatless roast made
and stuffed with God knows what.
She warned that Cousin Al
loves to initiate dinner conversation
in which he loudly expounds
on the abysmal state of the nation.

I thought, good grief,
will I be the only normal person there,
who eats meat and wheat,
and drinks whatever's offered to share?
I said I'd go, and attend I did,
in spite of growing trepidation.
And at its end, I agreed it was
a delightful Thanksgiving celebration.

Christmas Jam

I've got a whole lot to gripe about this time of year,
when instead I'm expected to focus on good cheer.
There's too much to eat, goodies everywhere I look.
When I open the fridge, so many choices to cook!

What gift for friends who have all their hearts' desire?
Their needs all are met, there's nothing they require.
I troll though shops packed with enticing merchandise,
seeking useful things, or something unique they'll prize.

Instead, I'm sorely tempted to buy for myself
those lovely items beckoning from the shelf
that aren't displayed until Black Friday rolls around,
with Christmas carols playing in the background.

All those wonderful holiday concerts and plays
unfortunately packed into just a few days.
No chance to savor each before rushing to the next.
No time to rest and recharge, no wonder I'm stressed!

The relatives and friends who ignored me all year
want to spend "quality time" now holidays are here.
The holiday gilt and guilt abound at Christmastime
in a season that should be serene and sublime.

I'm so blessed to live in the fullness of prosperity,
it should be easy to view this season with clarity.
My gripes and complaints are simply the voices
of having an abundance of wonderful choices.

Letter to Santa

Santa is coming to my neighborhood
and I'm afraid he knows I haven't been good.
I've stolen kisses and hugs and many a sly look,
and I know it's recorded in his big ole book.

I'll send Santa a list of all my good works
and hope he'll decide to overlook my quirks.
At church I've cooked and fed people soup;
at the cat shelter I've cleaned and scooped.

Is it too late now to submit my claim
that I'm really a good girl, just the same?
I only acted out of my heart's true feeling
'cause one certain man sets my mind reeling.

I love him to bits, he makes my heart quiver.
Santa, the very best gift you could deliver
is his love and devotion so we'd never part.
Oh, and please bring his body along with his heart.

Christmas Surprise

It's Christmas morning, and as I awake,
I see my backyard has become a lake.
A water feature wasn't my request this year
And I'm not quite sure how it got here.

Santa, did you do this thing to me?
Did you and all eight reindeer pee?
Did every snowman ever built
Come over to my backyard to melt?

I went out and took a closer look.
Guess I've gotta let Santa off the hook,
For there gushing boldly in front of me
Was a broken water pipe of PVC.

Instead of relaxing on Christmas Day,
I'll be feverishly slaving away.
Mud to my knees, water to my hips.
It won't be Christmas carols rolling off my lips!

Mrs. C.'s Funeral

It was an old fashion funeral
with a casket and wreaths of flowers.
As Mrs. C. lay in quiet repose,
the service went on for hours.

When at last the formalities ended,
and time for visiting had begun,
the mourners compared their illnesses.
It seemed Mrs. C. was the healthiest one.

She certainly appeared more calm,
relaxed and happier than those standing,
enthusiastically competing to see
whose funeral next they'll be attending.

Wearable Hugs

When my mother-in-law passed away,
I inherited her fuzzy pink bathrobe.
Now worn and frayed beyond usefulness,
it remains in the back of my closet
for dark days of emotional emergency.

My sister-by-choice passed away,
and I was given her thermal ski shirts.
Every winter at her favorite resort,
warmed by one of her shirts,
I dedicate a run to her and feel her joy.

A dear and much-admired friend just passed,
and I gladly accepted one of her cycling shirts.
Keeping her presence alive on the bike trails
we both enjoyed gives me pleasure and keeps her near.

Each time I snuggle into one of these garments,
it's like wearing a hug from someone I love.

Remembrance

My friend has gone from this earth,
gone to a place of peace and light.
Fitting, because she embodied peace, light,
kindness, caring and thoughtfulness
in all she did, in all she was.

No unkind word crossed her lips,
no jealousy colored green her world.
Her intrinsic nature was loving kindness
that radiated to everyone she knew,
whether for a lifetime or for only a moment.

I will honor my friend's too-brief life
by striving every day to emulate those attributes
I so admired in her
until they become reflexive in me,
my true nature as they were hers.

Thank you, Carol, for your example.
I wish I had told you before it was too late.
You were so optimistic, brave and courageous,
I could not accept that you were leaving.

Section VI

The Spirituality of An Ordinary Life

Was That You, God?

I wrote what was in my heart last night,
not really believing in its worth.
Just nocturnal musings of an ordinary human
sifting through human emotions.
With no confidence in its value,
I wrote on the back of a discarded envelope.
In the morning, I was awestruck.
How could *I* have written something so profound?
I think it was not me at all.
Was that you, God?

God's Kite

I am a kite, borne on the breath of God,
soaring ever higher in luminous glory.
No matter where my feet have trod,
sky bound, I'm writing a brand new story.

I do not sit and wait for the breeze to lift me.
Enlivened by passion and joyful abandon
I run headlong into life with expectant glee,
trusting my tether is secure in God's hand.

This trust gives me freedom to fly, to grow,
though clouds may appear and storms may threaten.
I plan, I decide how my life should go;
then God's breezes blow in a different direction.

Not designed to lay motionless in the dust,
I lift up with a clear mind and a light heart.
Like a paper kite that welcomes the gust,
I trust the flight of life and enjoy my earthly part.

Personal GPS

Just in case Siri does not know everything,
you're equipped with a personal GPS,
downloaded into the center of your heart
to assure your life's journey will meet success.

When the world is shouting, "No you can't!"
but your heart guide softly whispers, "Yes,"
pay no attention to the outer world's chatter
and faithfully follow your personal GPS.

That's where your true direction is found,
if you'll pay attention while you roam.
No matter how winding the road may be,
this GPS will always guide you safely home.

What Is God?

If all songs sounded the same,
they couldn't express the range of human emotions.
The same prayer won't do for every situation, either,
and the way I envision God changes, too.

Most of the time, I think of God as Spirit,
an all-encompassing energy that permeates
all aspects of life, filling all of time and space,
the molecules of my body, and the air I breathe.

But when I need the comfort of a warm hug,
I experience God as a loving parent,
sometimes a mother, sometimes a father,
with a kindly countenance and arms to hold me close.

I don't think God cares how we image Him,
or Her, or It; or the name we use for God;
but cares only that we seek His wisdom, Her love,
and Its presence in our daily lives.

Beginner's Mind

The Beginner's Mind allows us to start anew,
begin again anytime, refresh, relax and renew.
To release the unhelpful patterns of yesterday
and begin to see there's a more productive way
to approach situations which seem intractable,
or resolve conflicts in ways more practical
than ended friendships, mayhem, or divorce.
The Beginner's Mind can make a different choice.

The Beginner's Mind frees us from doubt and fear
and lets Spirit's wisdom make the path clear
to forgiving ourselves and those who hurt us,
sweeping away the internal chatter and fuss.
The Beginner's Mind is open, innocent and receptive,
listening intently for Spirit's whispered directive.
Spirit's plans and dreams for us are always higher
than the best of what we alone imagine or desire.

Truth or Fiction

"Truth is sometimes best expressed outside the limited realm of facts." - Rev. Tom Thorpe

There is a reason art
and music and poetry exist.
Some things are understood only
in the realm of the heart.
Our minds attempt to grasp meaning,
with all its twists,
but it's within our hearts
that truth and fiction stand apart.

The heart sees and hears and knows
without need of facts
the truth Spirit makes known
to those who are willing to heed.
When confronted with conflicting beliefs,
it's best to relax
and allow knowing from within,
intellect keen, yet freed.

In spite of preconceived notions
and dogma set in stone,
wisdom flows into open hearts
at moments most unlikely,
lifting us to higher states of consciousness
than we have known
if we do not hold to cherished beliefs
and old stories too tightly.

Truth is not always in appearances,
facts, or mathematical equations,
but lodged among all those,
between the lines written on the pages,
waiting to be accepted,
revealed, on unexpected occasions.
It's why humanity treasures artists
and mystics throughout the ages.

The Forest of My Mind

I walked serenely through a meadow,
the path well-marked and wide,
confident and happy,
enjoying wildflowers on either side.
The path turned into the woods
and suddenly disappeared,
leaving me feeling lost
and wondering where to go from here.

Behind me the path I'd walked
was nowhere to be found,
and no direction looked inviting
as I turned to glance around.
I sat down on a log to think,
and very soon began to pray
that my dear guardian angel
would come show me the way.

Although no angel appeared
out of the forest or the blue,
I felt a nudge of intuition
tell me what to do.

I thought about challenges
I've already overturned
and asked myself how I could
apply what I had learned.

The answer came in a sudden flash
of certain inner knowing:
I am never really lost at all,
for God knows where I'm going.
In the past when disaster struck,
I'd get angry and brood.
But challenges already met
increased my fortitude.

Now light of heart and light of step,
my confidence renewed,
I can find my way through
life's dark forests with certitude.
Next time I feel alone and lost,
and don't know where to turn,
I'll seek opportunity instead
of focusing on my concern.

Section VII

Just for Grins

Temptation

I steeled myself as I prepared to walk by
their warm and enticing invitation.
Today I vowed to be brave and strong
and not indulge in wicked flirtation.

I would not give in, I told myself sternly,
as around the fateful corner I turned.
I would not give them a second glance,
with their appeal I'd be unconcerned.

Then the devil made me do it,
break all my resolve and yield.
I went in and bought half a dozen
chocolate chunk cookies from Mrs. Field.

An Ode to Dust

I must learn to love Dust.
It is a loyal and trustworthy companion.
It will never leave me of its own volition.
It will tolerate abuse and return again and again,
devotedly offering itself to me.
No matter how many times I attempt to eliminate it with
rags, feathers, or vacuum, lo, it returns, coating every still
surface, creeping into every crevice, every nook and
cranny, lest I be bereft of its company and perish in
loneliness.

Oh, Noble Dust, to find a friend with your steadfastness.
A friend who will excuse, as you do, my casual
unconcern as you lie in dormant, expectant wait
for my attention.
A friend who will return, time and again, undaunted by
my efforts to annihilate him, to eradicate him from my
surroundings, from my very existence, for you
understand and express true love better than I.
And love me you do. You cling to me, and all
that is mine.
A friend with your constancy. You offer no surprises; I
know always what to expect from you.

Oh, Dust, forgive me! Forgive my zealous efforts
to avoid communion with you.
Forgive my cursing your existence,
my cruel smashing of your very atoms.
And tell me, if I embrace you,
will you become a Prince?
A Prince with your gentle, loving attributes?

Perhaps that is too great an expectation.
Perhaps I will write an Ode to Wine.

Catatonic

"Catatonic" is such a funny-sounding word.
The images it conjures up are really quite absurd.
Kitties sprawled all about in poses unaccustomed,
as if waiting for a catopractor
to come in and adjust 'em.

The Daze of My Lies

I'm a sexy size four who eats whatever she chooses.
With my true love by my side, my happiness oozes.
My genius kids graduated Stanford cum laude.
I can't even keep track of all my travels abroad.

The house stays clean with no effort of mine.
The yard's always green and looks perfectly fine.
The pantry's well-stocked, I entertain in a flash
anyone's small army without batting an eyelash.

I wear diamonds and Gucci without seeming haughty
as I drive to buy groceries in my new Maserati.
I have so much money there's nothing I can't buy.
And my neighbor's pigs have just learned how to fly.

Woman's Work is Never Done

Why wasn't I born a princess,
not knowing what a dust rag is for?
In a family spoiled and privileged,
I'd never have to mop the floor.

Dark thoughts about my ancestry
cross my fevered mind as I toil.
I'm the only one here and the question is,
who brought in all this damn soil?

Cat in the Windowsill

When windowsills were first designed,
did the designer have in mind
they must accommodate a cat's behind?

No matter how wide the cat,
or how narrow the windowsill,
if the cat wants to sit on that,
it will.

Ideal Dinner Party

Everyone came to the campfire I hosted.
Hot dogs and marshmallows on sticks they roasted.
The party ended as every hostess wishes:
They did the cooking, I'll burn the dishes.

Cajun Tom

He play Cajun fiddle
Lithe, lean, sensuous
Move like cat
Throw back head
Sing out loud
He gots no butt
What he sit on?

www.ingramcontent.com/pod-product-compliance
Lightning Source LLC
Chambersburg PA
CBHW060849050426
42453CB00008B/908